Editor in Chief
Karen J. Goldfluss, M.S. Ed.

Creative Director
Sarah M. Fournier

Cover Artist
Sarah Kim

Imaging
Amanda R. Harter

Illustrator
Kelly McMahon

Publisher
Mary D. Smith, M.S. Ed.

10 Sight Words

1. Strengthens each student's ability to identify, understand, and use common sight words

2. Develops and reinforces correct spelling and word formation

3. Includes flash cards of words for practice opportunities

Teacher Created Resources

TCR 8059

Author
Erica N. Russikoff, M.A.

Teacher Created Resources
12621 Western Avenue
Garden Grove, CA 92841
www.teachercreated.com

ISBN: 978-1-4206-8059-1

©2018 Teacher Created Resources
Reprinted, 2019
Made in U.S.A.

Teacher Created Resources

Table of Contents

Introduction

Sight words are the most frequently used words in reading and writing. They are called "sight words" because they must be recognized instantly, on sight, for reading fluency. Many sight words do not follow standard phonics rules or spelling patterns, which makes them difficult for early readers to recognize, sound out, and comprehend. In this book, 100 sight words are provided for practice. Words 1–50 are intended for first-grade students, while words 51–100 are intended for second-grade students. The words are organized by Dr. Fry's order of frequency, with the word *will* being the most frequently used word in the English language. The words can be taught sequentially, but, depending on what an individual student needs, a teacher can choose to skip some words or teach some words before others.

Each word is introduced and taught individually. A series of exercises develops, reinforces, and strengthens students' ability to do the following:

- follow directions

- recognize the words on sight

- write the words with proper letter formation

- identify the letters in the words

- write the words with correct spelling

- use the written-out words in sentences

Additional activities, starting on page 105, encourage students to choose the correct sight word from two choices. All of the answer choices (sight words) can be found in this book. These activities provide extra practice for students who are familiar with sight words and want to continue their learning.

The flash cards at the back of this book can be used for reinforcement and testing. Consider punching holes through them so that the cards can be held together by a string or binder ring.

The activities in this book have been aligned to the Common Core State Standards for Language Arts. These standards can be found on the last page of this book.

How to Use This Book

The following exercises are included in this book:

Tracing and Writing the Word

This activity allows students to recognize a new sight word. When students trace a word, they become familiar with the letters and sequence that make up the new word. This activity also invites students to practice their letter formation.

Identifying the Word in a Group

This activity requires students to choose the new sight word from amongst other similarly spelled or similar sounding words. In doing so, students are learning to distinguish the word from other common words.

Circling the Word's Vowels

This activity reinforces the idea that language has rules. Every word requires at least one vowel. Learning which vowels are in which words will help students later when they experience phonics, syllabication, and spelling exercises.

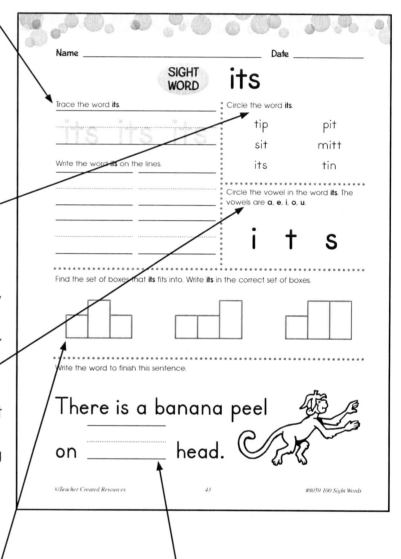

Finding the Box the Word Fits Into

This activity allows students to focus on the shape of the new sight word. It invites students to think about how the letters fit against each other—whether letters go above or below the line and whether those upward or downward letters go at the beginning or end of the word.

Writing the Word in a Sentence

This activity encourages students to practice writing the new sight word in a sentence. The sentence includes the sight word with a related picture. *Note:* Sometimes the word is used at the beginning of the sentence. (See page 5 for an example.) In these cases, the capital letter will need to be taught and practiced.

SIGHT WORD

will

Trace the word **will**.

~~will~~   ~~will~~

Write the word **will** on the lines.

_____   _____

_____   _____

_____   _____

Circle the word **will**.

we   fill

will   win

bill   hill

Circle the vowel in the word **will**. The vowels are **a**, **e**, **i**, **o**, **u**.

w   i   l   l

Find the set of boxes that **will** fits into. Write **will** in the correct set of boxes.

Write the word to finish this sentence.

_____ you

wear the jacket?

Name _____   Date _____

SIGHT WORD

up

Trace the word **up**.

....

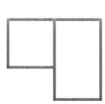 up   up   up

....

Write the word **up** on the lines.

_____   _____

....
_____   _____

....
_____   _____

Circle the word **up**.

help   up

us   pin

pull   pill

Circle the vowel in the word **up**. The vowels are **a, e, i, o, u.**

 u   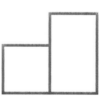 p

Find the set of boxes that **up** fits into. Write **up** in the correct set of boxes.

Write the word to finish this sentence.

_____
....
Go _____ the

ladder.

SIGHT WORD

other

Trace the word **other**.

other other

Write the word **other** on the lines.

Circle the word **other**.

other	otter
pot	this
then	both

Circle the vowels in the word **other**.
The vowels are **a, e, i, o, u**.

o t h e r

Find the set of boxes that **other** fits into. Write **other** in the correct set of boxes.

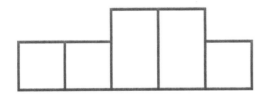 

Write the word to finish this sentence.

I live on the

_____

_____ side.

Name _____   Date _____

SIGHT WORD
about

Trace the word **about**.

about about

Write the word **about** on the lines.

_____   _____

_____   _____

_____   _____

Circle the word **about**.

bat   town

bound   about

boat   but

Circle the vowels in the word **about**.
The vowels are **a, e, i, o, u**.

a b o u t

Find the set of boxes that **about** fits into. Write **about** in the correct set of boxes.

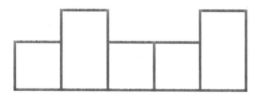   

Write the word to finish this sentence.

What do you know

_____

_____ money?

Name _____   Date _____

SIGHT WORD

out

Trace the word **out**.

out   out

Write the word **out** on the lines.

Circle the word **out**.

ton	of
too	two
out	on

Circle the vowels in the word **out**. The vowels are **a, e, i, o, u**.

o   u   t

Find the set of boxes that **out** fits into. Write **out** in the correct set of boxes.

Write the word to finish this sentence.

Watch _____

for the crab!

Name _____ Date _____

SIGHT WORD

many

Trace the word **many**.

many many

Write the word **many** on the lines.

_____ _____

_____ _____

_____ _____

Circle the word **many**.

many   way

money   wary

men   nanny

Circle the vowels in the word **many**. The vowels are **a**, **e**, **i**, **o**, **u**, and sometimes **y**.

m a n y

Find the set of boxes that **many** fits into. Write **many** in the correct set of boxes.

Write the word to finish this sentence.

I made _____

cookies.

Name _____   Date _____

SIGHT WORD

then

Trace the word **then**.

then then

Write the word **then** on the lines.

Circle the word **then**.

them	than
then	ten
thing	hand

Circle the vowel in the word **then**. The vowels are **a**, **e**, **i**, **o**, **u**.

t h e n

Find the set of boxes that **then** fits into. Write **then** in the correct set of boxes.

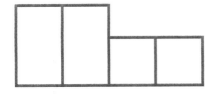 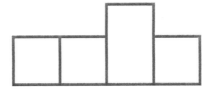 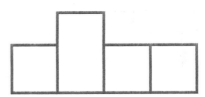

Write the word to finish this sentence.

They hiked _____

_____ ate.

SIGHT WORD

them

Trace the word **them**.

them them

Write the word **them** on the lines.

_____ _____

_____ _____

_____ _____

Circle the word **them**.

thank   hen

then   them

think   ham

Circle the vowel in the word **them**.
The vowels are **a**, **e**, **i**, **o**, **u**.

t h e m

Find the set of boxes that **them** fits into. Write **them** in the correct set of boxes.

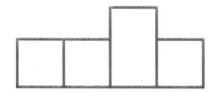  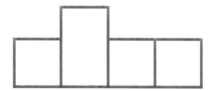

Write the word to finish this sentence.

She loves

_____

_____ .

SIGHT WORD

these

Trace the word **these**.

these these

Write the word **these** on the lines.

_____   _____

_____   _____

_____   _____

_____   _____

Circle the word **these**.

this   then

please   them

these   has

Circle the vowels in the word **these**. The vowels are **a, e, i, o, u**.

t h e s e

Find the set of boxes that **these** fits into. Write **these** in the correct set of boxes.

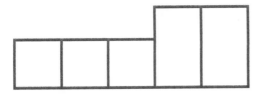   

Write the word to finish this sentence.

_____

_____ bugs

have legs.

Name _____   Date _____

SIGHT WORD   # SO

Trace the word **so**.

....

so   so   so

....

Write the word **so** on the lines.

_____   _____

_____   _____

_____   _____

_____   _____

Circle the word **so**.

sew   so

see   most

is   nose

Circle the vowel in the word **so**. The vowels are **a, e, i, o, u**.

S   O

Find the set of boxes that **so** fits into. Write **so** in the correct set of boxes.

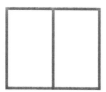   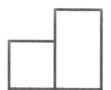   

Write the word to finish this sentence.

It's _____ early!

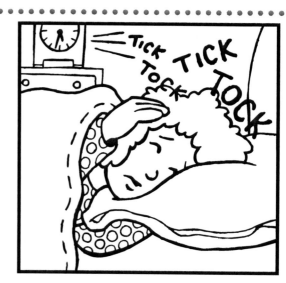

SIGHT WORD

some

Trace the word **some**.

some some

Write the word **some** on the lines.

_____   _____

_____   _____

_____   _____

Circle the word **some**.

sun   come

sum   gone

some   dome

Circle the vowels in the word **some**.
The vowels are **a**, **e**, **i**, **o**, **u**.

s o m e

Find the set of boxes that **some** fits into. Write **some** in the correct set of boxes.

Write the word to finish this sentence.

Throw _____

dice.

Name _____ Date _____

SIGHT WORD ## her

Trace the word **her**.

her   her

Write the word **her** on the lines.

_____ _____

_____ _____

_____ _____

Circle the word **her**.

hen   hurt

hair   horn

hare   her

Circle the vowel in the word **her**. The vowels are **a**, **e**, **i**, **o**, **u**.

h   e   r

Find the set of boxes that **her** fits into. Write **her** in the correct set of boxes.

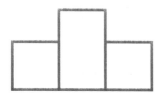   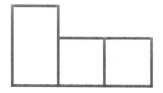   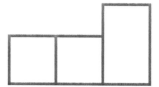

Write the word to finish this sentence.

She is washing

_____

_____ hands.

Name _____ Date _____

SIGHT WORD # would

Trace the word **would**.

would would

Write the word **would** on the lines.

_____ _____

Circle the word **would**.

could   would

should   wood

wool   won

Circle the vowels in the word **would**.
The vowels are **a**, **e**, **i**, **o**, **u**.

would

Find the set of boxes that **would** fits into. Write **would** in the correct set of boxes.

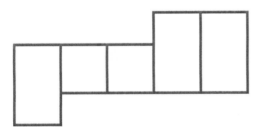

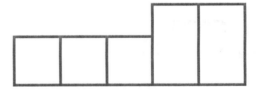

Write the word to finish this sentence.

_____

_____ you

like some honey?

Name _____ Date _____

make

Trace the word **make**.

make make

Write the word **make** on the lines.

_____ _____

_____ _____

_____ _____

Circle the word **make**.

cake   made

make   mad

bake   take

Circle the vowels in the word **make**.
The vowels are **a**, **e**, **i**, **o**, **u**.

m a k e

Find the set of boxes that **make** fits into. Write **make** in the correct set of boxes.

Write the word to finish this sentence.

Can you _____ this?

SIGHT WORD

like

Trace the word **like**.

like   like

Write the word **like** on the lines.

Circle the word **like**.

like	look
lick	lie
bike	hike

Circle the vowels in the word **like**. The vowels are **a, e, i, o, u**.

l i k e

Find the set of boxes that **like** fits into. Write **like** in the correct set of boxes.

Write the word to finish this sentence.

I _____ to dance.

Name _____ Date _____

SIGHT WORD

him

Trace the word **him**.

him him

Write the word **him** on the lines.

Circle the word **him**.

hit dim

his rim

him hen

Circle the vowel in the word **him**. The vowels are **a, e, i, o, u**.

h i m

Find the set of boxes that **him** fits into. Write **him** in the correct set of boxes.

Write the word to finish this sentence.

Look at _____ hop!

SIGHT WORD

into

Trace the word **into**.

into   into

Write the word **into** on the lines.

Circle the word **into**.

into	lint
in	mint
hint	ton

Circle the vowels in the word **into**. The vowels are **a**, **e**, **i**, **o**, **u**.

i n t o

Find the set of boxes that **into** fits into. Write **into** in the correct set of boxes.

Write the word to finish this sentence.

Go _____

the house.

Name _____ **Date** _____

SIGHT WORD

time

Trace the word **time**.

time   time

Write the word **time** on the lines.

_____   _____

_____   _____

_____   _____

Circle the word **time**.

mime	mit
dime	time
tine	met

Circle the vowels in the word **time**. The vowels are **a, e, i, o, u**.

t i m e

Find the set of boxes that **time** fits into. Write **time** in the correct set of boxes.

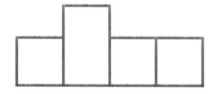
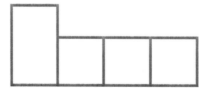
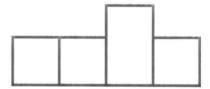

Write the word to finish this sentence.

It's _____

to clean!

Name _____   Date _____

SIGHT WORD

has

Trace the word **has**.

. . . .

~~has~~   ~~has~~

Write the word **has** on the lines.

_____   _____

_____   _____

_____   _____

Circle the word **has**.

gas   last

fast   past

has   his

Circle the vowel in the word **has**. The vowels are **a, e, i, o, u.**

h   a   s

Find the set of boxes that **has** fits into. Write **has** in the correct set of boxes.

Write the word to finish this sentence.

She _____ many

books.

Name _____ Date _____

SIGHT WORD look

Trace the word **look**.

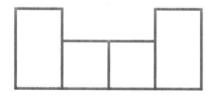

Write the word **look** on the lines.

Circle the word **look**.

cook   cool

like   book

lost   look

Circle the vowels in the word **look**.
The vowels are **a, e, i, o, u**.

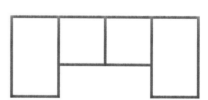

Find the set of boxes that **look** fits into. Write **look** in the correct set of boxes.

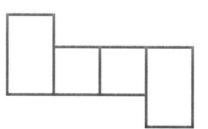

Write the word to finish this sentence.

_____ at

that star!

SIGHT WORD

two

Trace the word **two**.

two   two

Write the word **two** on the lines.

Circle the word **two**.

won   tow

two   wit

too   won

Circle the vowel in the word **two**. The vowels are **a, e, i, o, u.**

t   w   o

Find the set of boxes that **two** fits into. Write **two** in the correct set of boxes.

Write the word to finish this sentence.

There are _____

crayons.

SIGHT WORD

more

Trace the word **more**.

more more

Write the word **more** on the lines.

Circle the word **more**.

mode   more

make   most

man   mop

Circle the vowels in the word **more**.
The vowels are **a**, **e**, **i**, **o**, **u**.

m o r e

Find the set of boxes that **more** fits into. Write **more** in the correct set of boxes.

Write the word to finish this sentence.

Who is having

_____

fun?

Name _____   Date _____

SIGHT WORD   # write

Trace the word **write**.

write write

Write the word **write** on the lines.

_____ _____

_____ _____

_____ _____

Circle the word **write**.

write	right
wit	will
bite	white

Circle the vowels in the word **write**. The vowels are **a**, **e**, **i**, **o**, **u**.

w r i t e

Find the set of boxes that **write** fits into. Write **write** in the correct set of boxes.

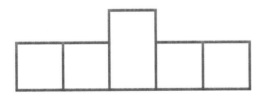 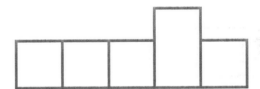

Write the word to finish this sentence.

What will you
_____
_____ ?

Name _____   Date _____

SIGHT WORD

go

Trace the word **go**.

go go go

Write the word **go** on the lines.

_____ _____

_____ _____

_____ _____

_____ _____

Circle the word **go**.

fog	gag
dog	get
log	go

Circle the vowel in the word **go**. The vowels are **a, e, i, o, u.**

g   o

Find the set of boxes that **go** fits into. Write **go** in the correct set of boxes.

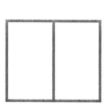   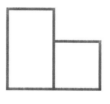   

Write the word to finish this sentence.

Let's _____ fly

a kite.

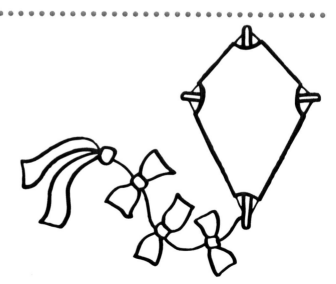

Name _____   Date _____

see

Trace the word **see**.

see   see

Write the word **see** on the lines.

Circle the word **see**.

me   see

bee   sea

tea   seat

Circle the vowels in the word **see**. The vowels are **a, e, i, o, u**.

s   e   e

Find the set of boxes that **see** fits into. Write **see** in the correct set of boxes.

Write the word to finish this sentence.

He could _____

in the dark.

SIGHT WORD

number

Trace the word **number**.

number

Write the word **number** on the lines.

Circle the word **number**.

numb	burn
lumber	men
number	bun

Circle the vowels in the word **number**. The vowels are **a, e, i, o, u**.

number

Find the set of boxes that **number** fits into. Write **number** in the correct set of boxes.

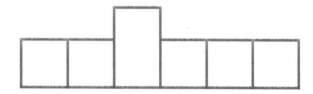

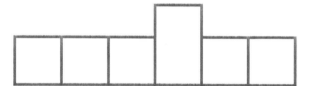

Write the word to finish this sentence.

Guess the

_____

of toys.

Name _____   Date _____

SIGHT WORD

no

Trace the word **no**.

no no no

Write the word **no** on the lines.

_____ _____

_____ _____

_____ _____

Circle the word **no**.

on   ton

no   son

net   won

Circle the vowel in the word **no**. The vowels are **a, e, i, o, u**.

n   o

Find the set of boxes that **no** fits into. Write **no** in the correct set of boxes.

Write the word to finish this sentence.

This dog has

_____

_____ water.

Name _____   Date _____

SIGHT WORD

way

Trace the word **way**.

~~~~~~~~~~~~~~~~~~~~~~~~~~~~~~~~~~~~

way   way

Write the word **way** on the lines.

_____   _____

_____   _____

_____   _____

Circle the word **way**.

bay   lay

hay   way

day   may

Circle the vowel in the word **way**. The vowels are **a, e, i, o, u.**

w   a   y

Find the set of boxes that **way** fits into. Write **way** in the correct set of boxes.

Write the word to finish this sentence.

_____

Which _____

should she go?

Name _____   Date _____

could

Trace the word **could**.

could could

Write the word **could** on the lines.

_____   _____
....
_____   _____
....
_____   _____

Circle the word **could**.

cold   cod

would   should

cool   could

Circle the vowels in the word **could**.
The vowels are **a**, **e**, **i**, **o**, **u**.

c o u l d

Find the set of boxes that **could** fits into. Write **could** in the correct set of boxes.

Write the word to finish this sentence.

_____
....
_____

she

be sick?

Name _____ Date _____

SIGH WORD

people

Trace the word **people**.

people

Write the word **people** on the lines.

Circle the word **people**.

peep   pop

people   pep

leap   peel

Circle the vowels in the word **people**.
The vowels are **a**, **e**, **i**, **o**, **u**.

p e o p l e

Find the set of boxes that **people** fits into. Write **people** in the correct set of boxes.

Write the word to finish this sentence.

Some _____

can sing.

SIGHT WORD

my

Trace the word **my**.

my my my

Write the word **my** on the lines.

_____   _____

_____   _____

_____   _____

_____   _____

Circle the word **my**.

my	may
mine	by
mice	cry

Circle the vowel in the word **my**. The vowels are **a**, **e**, **i**, **o**, **u**, and sometimes **y**.

m   y

Find the set of boxes that **my** fits into. Write **my** in the correct set of boxes.

Write the word to finish this sentence.

Do you like
_____

_____ shirt?

Name _____   Date _____

SIGHT WORD

than

Trace the word **than**.

than than

Write the word **than** on the lines.

_____   _____

_____   _____

_____   _____

Circle the word **than**.

think	thing
then	hand
than	hang

Circle the vowel in the word **than**. The vowels are **a, e, i, o, u.**

t h a n

Find the set of boxes that **than** fits into. Write **than** in the correct set of boxes.

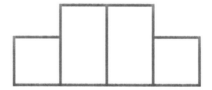

Write the word to finish this sentence.

There are more

_____

_____ four snails.

Name _____   Date _____

SIGHT WORD

first

Trace the word **first**.

first   first

Write the word **first** on the lines.

_____   _____

_____   _____

_____   _____

Circle the word **first**.

fish   first

fist   thirst

fig   worst

Circle the vowel in the word **first**. The vowels are **a, e, i, o, u.**

f i r s t

Find the set of boxes that **first** fits into. Write **first** in the correct set of boxes.

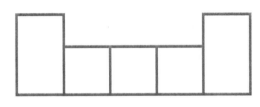   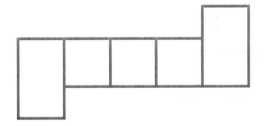

Write the word to finish this sentence.

_____
_____

he

dug a hole.

Name _____ **Date** _____

SIGHT WORD

water

Trace the word **water**.

water water

Write the word **water** on the lines.

_____ _____

_____ _____

_____ _____

Circle the word **water**.

matter   what

wear   water

wait   later

Circle the vowels in the word **water**.
The vowels are **a, e, i, o, u**.

w a t e r

Find the set of boxes that **water** fits into. Write **water** in the correct set of boxes.

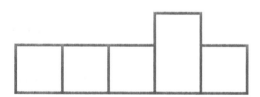 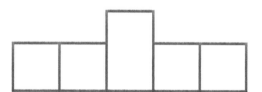

Write the word to finish this sentence.

Don't waste

_____

_____ .

Name _____   Date _____

SIGHT WORD   # been

Trace the word **been**.

been been

Write the word **been** on the lines.

_____ _____

_____ _____

Circle the word **been**.

bend	seen
bean	bin
been	teen

Circle the vowels in the word **been**.
The vowels are **a, e, i, o, u.**

b e e n

Find the set of boxes that **been** fits into. Write **been** in the correct set of boxes.

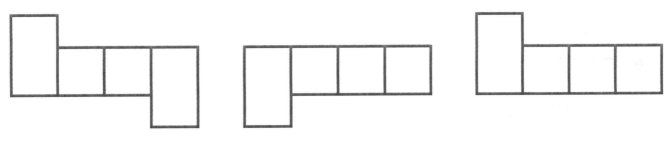

Write the word to finish this sentence.

Have you ever

_____

shopping?

Name _____ Date _____

SIGHT WORD

called

Trace the word **called**.

called called

Write the word **called** on the lines.

_____

_____

_____

_____

Circle the word **called**.

wall   calm

cold   came

balled   called

Circle the vowels in the word **called**.
The vowels are **a**, **e**, **i**, **o**, **u**.

called

Find the set of boxes that **called** fits into. Write **called** in the correct set of boxes.

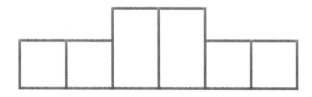 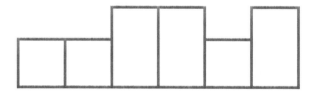

Write the word to finish this sentence.

He _____

her to say hi.

SIGHT WORD

who

Trace the word **who**.

who   who

Write the word **who** on the lines.

_____   _____

_____   _____

_____   _____

Circle the word **who**.

hoot   word

who   how

won   when

Circle the vowel in the word **who**. The vowels are **a**, **e**, **i**, **o**, **u**.

w h o

Find the set of boxes that **who** fits into. Write **who** in the correct set of boxes.

Write the word to finish this sentence.

_____ do you see?

Name _____   Date _____

SIGHT WORD

am

Trace the word **am**.

am am am

Write the word **am** on the lines.

_____   _____

_____   _____

_____   _____

Circle the word **am**.

am   an

man   map

pan   and

Circle the vowel in the word **am**. The vowels are **a, e, i, o, u**.

a   m

Find the set of boxes that **am** fits into. Write **am** in the correct set of boxes.

Write the word to finish this sentence.

I _____ listening

to my heart.

Name _____ Date _____

SIGHT WORD   **its**

Trace the word **its**.

its its its

Write the word **its** on the lines.

_____ _____

Circle the word **its**.

tip	pit
sit	mitt
its	tin

Circle the vowel in the word **its**. The vowels are **a, e, i, o, u.**

i t s

Find the set of boxes that **its** fits into. Write **its** in the correct set of boxes.

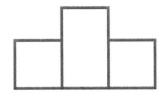  

Write the word to finish this sentence.

There is a banana peel _____

on _____ head.

Name _____ Date _____

SIGHT WORD # now

Trace the word **now**.

now   now

Write the word **now** on the lines.

_____   _____

_____   _____

_____   _____

Circle the word **now**.

won   now

not   win

nod   nose

Circle the vowel in the word **now**. The vowels are **a**, **e**, **i**, **o**, **u**.

n   o   w

Find the set of boxes that **now** fits into. Write **now** in the correct set of boxes.

Write the word to finish this sentence.

_____ he can

find it.

Name _____   Date _____

SIGHT WORD

find

Trace the word **find**.

find   find

Write the word **find** on the lines.

_____   _____

_____   _____

_____   _____

_____   _____

Circle the word **find**.

find   bind

wind   fine

vine   kind

Circle the vowel in the word **find**. The vowels are **a, e, i, o, u.**

f i n d

Find the set of boxes that **find** fits into. Write **find** in the correct set of boxes.

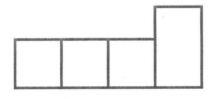 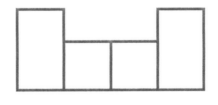 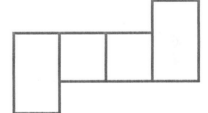

Write the word to finish this sentence.

Will he _____ her?

Name _____ Date _____

SIGHT WORD

long

Trace the word **long**.

long long

Write the word **long** on the lines.

_____ _____

Circle the word **long**.

ding   long

gone   song

log   hang

Circle the vowel in the word **long**. The vowels are **a, e, i, o, u**.

l o n g

Find the set of boxes that **long** fits into. Write **long** in the correct set of boxes.

Write the word to finish this sentence.

How _____

is the snake?

Name _____   Date _____

SIGHT WORD # down

Trace the word **down**.

down down

Write the word **down** on the lines.

Circle the word **down**.

won   clown

nod   now

town   down

Circle the vowel in the word **down**.
The vowels are **a**, **e**, **i**, **o**, **u**.

d o w n

Find the set of boxes that **down** fits into. Write **down** in the correct set of boxes.

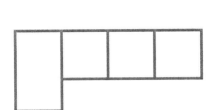 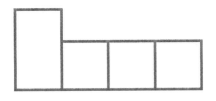 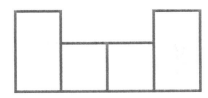

Write the word to finish this sentence.

The mouse ran

_____

the clock.

SIGHT WORD

day

Trace the word **day**.

day   day

Write the word **day** on the lines.

_____   _____

_____   _____

_____   _____

Circle the word **day**.

dam	hay
may	day
say	dawn

Circle the vowel in the word **day**. The vowels are **a, e, i, o, u**.

d a y

Find the set of boxes that **day** fits into. Write **day** in the correct set of boxes.

Write the word to finish this sentence.

It is a new _____!

Name _____   Date _____

SIGHT WORD   # did

Trace the word **did**.

did   did

Write the word **did** on the lines.

_____   _____

Circle the word **did**.

dud   dig

did   dip

dim   dirt

Circle the vowel in the word **did**. The vowels are **a, e, i, o, u**.

d   i   d

Find the set of boxes that **did** fits into. Write **did** in the correct set of boxes.

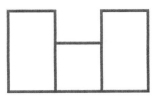   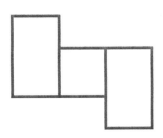   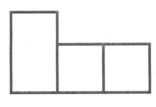

Write the word to finish this sentence.

What _____ you

make for dinner?

Name _____   Date _____

SIGHT WORD

get

Trace the word **get**.

get   get

Write the word **get** on the lines.

_____   _____

_____   _____

_____   _____

Circle the word **get**.

got   tag

gate   gut

get   tug

Circle the vowel in the word **get**. The vowels are **a, e, i, o, u**.

g   e   t

Find the set of boxes that **get** fits into. Write **get** in the correct set of boxes.

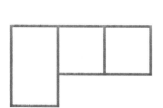 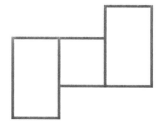 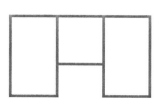

Write the word to finish this sentence.

Can we _____ one?

SIGHT WORD

come

Trace the word **come**.

come come

Write the word **come** on the lines.

_____ _____

_____ _____

_____ _____

Circle the word **come**.

come	more
came	mice
cone	dome

Circle the vowels in the word **come**.
The vowels are **a**, **e**, **i**, **o**, **u**.

c o m e

Find the set of boxes that **come** fits into. Write **come** in the correct set of boxes.

Write the word to finish this sentence.

_____

_____

look at them!

Name _____   Date _____

SIGHT WORD

made

Trace the word **made**.

made made

Write the word **made** on the lines.

_____   _____

_____   _____

_____   _____

_____   _____

Circle the word **made**.

mane   make

maze   mad

maid   made

Circle the vowels in the word **made**.
The vowels are **a**, **e**, **i**, **o**, **u**.

m a d e

Find the set of boxes that **made** fits into. Write **made** in the correct set of boxes.

Write the word to finish this sentence.

Look at what I

_____

_____ !

SIGHT WORD

may

Trace the word **may**.

may may

Write the word **may** on the lines.

Circle the word **may**.

my	may
yam	mad
man	day

Circle the vowel in the word **may**. The vowels are **a**, **e**, **i**, **o**, **u**.

m a y

Find the set of boxes that **may** fits into. Write **may** in the correct set of boxes.

Write the word to finish this sentence.

He _____ need some help.

SIGHT WORD

part

Trace the word **part**.

part part

Write the word **part** on the lines.

_____   _____

_____   _____

_____   _____

Circle the word **part**.

park   pear

cart   part

heart   tarp

Circle the vowel in the word **part**. The vowels are **a, e, i, o, u**.

p a r t

Find the set of boxes that **part** fits into. Write **part** in the correct set of boxes.

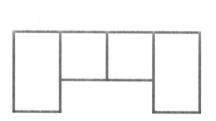 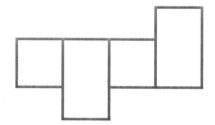 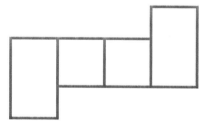

Write the word to finish this sentence.

Which _____ of the

snowman is missing?

Name _____ Date _____

SIGHT WORD

over

Trace the word **over**.

over over

Write the word **over** on the lines.

Circle the word **over**.

oven   dove

over   move

river   cove

Circle the vowels in the word **over**.
The vowels are **a**, **e**, **i**, **o**, **u**.

o v e r

Find the set of boxes that **over** fits into. Write **over** in the correct set of boxes.

Write the word to finish this sentence.

The ball went
_____
the fence.

Name _____   Date _____

SIGHT WORD   # new

Trace the word **new**.

new   new

Write the word **new** on the lines.

_____   _____

_____   _____

_____   _____

Circle the word **new**.

neck   net

when   men

new   went

Circle the vowel in the word **new**. The vowels are **a, e, i, o, u**.

n   e   w

Find the set of boxes that **new** fits into. Write **new** in the correct set of boxes.

Write the word to finish this sentence.

These are my

_____

_____ shoes.

Name _____ Date _____

SIGHT WORD sound

Trace the word **sound**.

sound sound

Write the word **sound** on the lines.

_____ _____

_____ _____

_____ _____

Circle the word **sound**.

round	sun
mound	soon
found	sound

Circle the vowels in the word **sound**.
The vowels are **a, e, i, o, u.**

s o u n d

Find the set of boxes that **sound** fits into. Write **sound** in the correct set of boxes.

Write the word to finish this sentence.

What _____

does a crow make?

Name _____ Date _____

SIGHT WORD # take

Trace the word **take**.

take   take

Write the word **take** on the lines.

_____   _____

_____   _____

_____   _____

Circle the word **take**.

take   lake

cake   make

gate   tape

Circle the vowels in the word **take**.
The vowels are **a, e, i, o, u.**

t a k e

Find the set of boxes that **take** fits into. Write **take** in the correct set of boxes.

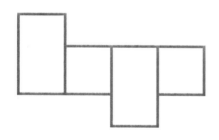 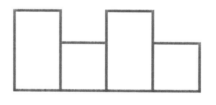 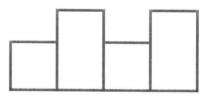

Write the word to finish this sentence.

_____

_____ a

spoonful.

Name _____   **Date** _____

SIGHT WORD

only

Trace the word **only**.

only only

Write the word **only** on the lines.

Circle the word **only**.

lonely	long
money	only
one	once

Circle the vowels in the word **only**. The vowels are **a**, **e**, **i**, **o**, **u**, and sometimes **y**.

o n l y

Find the set of boxes that **only** fits into. Write **only** in the correct set of boxes.

Write the word to finish this sentence.

I _____

have one dog.

Name _____   Date _____

little

Trace the word **little**.

little

Write the word **little** on the lines.

_____
_____
_____
_____

Circle the word **little**.

lit	little
tile	title
tell	let

Circle the vowels in the word **little**. The vowels are **a, e, i, o, u**.

l i t t l e

Find the set of boxes that **little** fits into. Write **little** in the correct set of boxes.

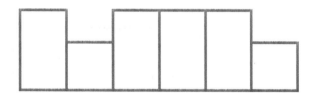   

Write the word to finish this sentence.

A _____

juice spilled.

Name _____ Date _____

SIGHT WORD

work

Trace the word **work**.

........work work........

Write the word **work** on the lines.

_____ _____

_____ _____

_____ _____

Circle the word **work**.

work	worm
fork	worn
wore	pork

Circle the vowel in the word **work**. The vowels are **a, e, i, o, u.**

w o r k

Find the set of boxes that **work** fits into. Write **work** in the correct set of boxes.

Write the word to finish this sentence.

I _____ at

a flower shop.

Name _____ Date _____

know

Trace the word know.

know know

Write the word know on the lines.

_____ _____

_____ _____

_____ _____

Circle the word know.

work   woke

won   honk

know   nook

Circle the vowel in the word know.
The vowels are a, e, i, o, u.

k n o w

Find the set of boxes that **know** fits into. Write **know** in the correct set of boxes.

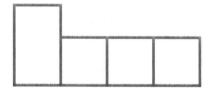 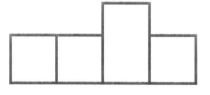 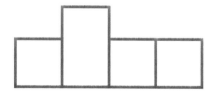

Write the word to finish this sentence.

What do you _____

about the ocean?

62   ©Teacher Created Resources

Name _____   Date _____

SIGHT WORD

place

Trace the word **place**.

place place

Write the word **place** on the lines.

Circle the word **place**.

pace   face

cape   place

lap   plane

Circle the vowels in the word **place**.
The vowels are **a**, **e**, **i**, **o**, **u**.

p l a c e

Find the set of boxes that **place** fits into. Write **place** in the correct set of boxes.

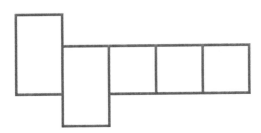 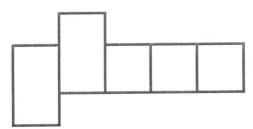

Write the word to finish this sentence.

Have you been to _____

this _____ ?

Name _____   Date _____

SIGHT WORD

years

Trace the word **years**.

....

~~years years~~

_____

Write the word **years** on the lines.

_____

....

_____

....

_____

Circle the word **years**.

tears	yes
years	says
fears	rays

Circle the vowels in the word **years**. The vowels are **a**, **e**, **i**, **o**, **u**.

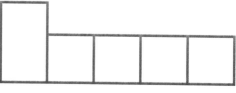

Find the set of boxes that **years** fits into. Write **years** in the correct set of boxes.

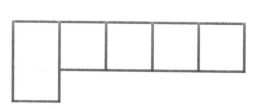

Write the word to finish this sentence.

This tree is twenty

_____

....

_____ old.

SIGHT WORD

live

Trace the word **live**.

live   live

Write the word **live** on the lines.

_____   _____

_____   _____

_____   _____

Circle the word **live**.

line   lid

leave   hive

dive   live

Circle the vowels in the word **live**. The vowels are **a, e, i, o, u**.

l i v e

Find the set of boxes that **live** fits into. Write **live** in the correct set of boxes.

Write the word to finish this sentence.

I _____ with

my baby sister.

Name _____   Date _____

SIGHT WORD me

Trace the word **me**.

me   me

Write the word **me** on the lines.

_____   _____

_____   _____

_____   _____

Circle the word **me**.

mat   me

man   mop

gem   my

Circle the vowel in the word **me**. The vowels are **a, e, i, o, u.**

m   e

Find the set of boxes that **me** fits into. Write **me** in the correct set of boxes.

Write the word to finish this sentence.

Follow _____ !

Name _____   Date _____

SIGHT WORD back

Trace the word **back**.

back back

Write the word **back** on the lines.

_____ _____

Circle the word **back**.

pack   ball

bag   back

sack   book

Circle the vowel in the word **back**.
The vowels are **a, e, i, o, u.**

b a c k

Find the set of boxes that **back** fits into. Write **back** in the correct set of boxes.

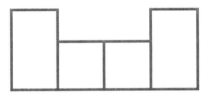 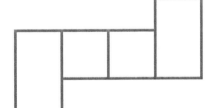 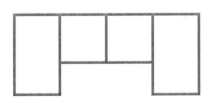

Write the word to finish this sentence.

I'm going _____

to sleep.

SIGH WORD

give

Trace the word **give**.

give   give

Write the word **give** on the lines.

_____   _____

_____   _____

_____   _____

Circle the word **give**.

glove   live

dive   gave

give   five

Circle the vowels in the word **give**.
The vowels are **a**, **e**, **i**, **o**, **u**.

g   i   v   e

Find the set of boxes that **give** fits into. Write **give** in the correct set of boxes.

Write the word to finish this sentence.

We can _____

you a ride.

Name _____ Date _____

SIGHT WORD # most

Trace the word **most**.

most most

Write the word **most** on the lines.

Circle the word **most**.

mist   post

most   must

lost   mast

Circle the vowel in the word **most**. The vowels are **a, e, i, o, u**.

m   o   s   t

Find the set of boxes that **most** fits into. Write **most** in the correct set of boxes.

Write the word to finish this sentence.

_____ kids

are happy.

Name _____ Date _____

SIGHT WORD

very

Trace the word **very**.

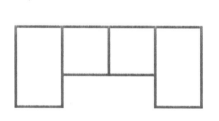

Write the word **very** on the lines.

_____ _____

_____ _____

_____ _____

Circle the word **very**.

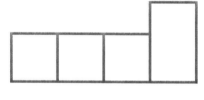

very   berry

cherry   verb

yes   yet

Circle the vowels in the word **very**. The vowels are **a**, **e**, **i**, **o**, **u**, and sometimes **y**.

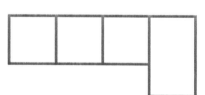

v e r y

Find the set of boxes that **very** fits into. Write **very** in the correct set of boxes.

Write the word to finish this sentence.

The dog is _____

_____ wet.

Name _____ Date _____

SIGHT WORD # after

Trace the word **after**.

after after

Write the word **after** on the lines.

_____ _____

_____ _____

_____ _____

Circle the word **after**.

raft   after

half   tear

later   alter

Circle the vowels in the word **after**. The vowels are **a**, **e**, **i**, **o**, **u**.

a f t e r

Find the set of boxes that **after** fits into. Write **after** in the correct set of boxes.

 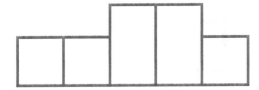

Write the word to finish this sentence.

She swam _____  diving into the pool.

Name _____ Date _____

things

Trace the word **things**.

things

Write the word **things** on the lines.

_____
_____
_____
_____

Circle the word **things**.

swings   brings

kings   thinks

sings   things

Circle the vowel in the word **things**.
The vowels are **a**, **e**, **i**, **o**, **u**.

things

Find the set of boxes that **things** fits into. Write **things** in the correct set of boxes.

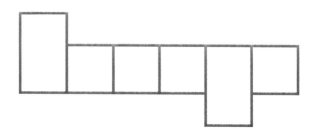 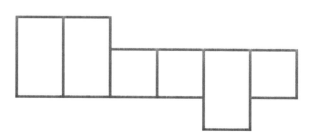

Write the word to finish this sentence.

I like to grow

_____ .

SIGHT WORD

our

Trace the word **our**.

our   our

Write the word **our** on the lines.

Circle the word **our**.

out   or

own   on

our   owe

Circle the vowels in the word **our**. The vowels are **a, e, i, o, u**.

o   u   r

Find the set of boxes that **our** fits into. Write **our** in the correct set of boxes.

Write the word to finish this sentence.

Do you like

_____

_____ hats?

Name _____ Date _____

SIGHT WORD

just

Trace the word **just**.

just just

Write the word **just** on the lines.

_____ _____

_____ _____

_____ _____

Circle the word **just**.

just   must

gust   dust

rust   bus

Circle the vowel in the word **just**. The vowels are **a, e, i, o, u**.

j u s t

Find the set of boxes that **just** fits into. Write **just** in the correct set of boxes.

Write the word to finish this sentence.

She _____

turned the light off.

SIGHT WORD

name

Trace the word **name**.

name name

Write the word **name** on the lines.

Circle the word **name**.

came   game

same   name

mean   nine

Circle the vowels in the word **name**.
The vowels are **a, e, i, o, u**.

n a m e

Find the set of boxes that **name** fits into. Write **name** in the correct set of boxes.

Write the word to finish this sentence.

Write your

_____.

Name _____ Date _____

SIGHT WORD

good

Trace the word **good**.

good good

Write the word **good** on the lines.

_____ _____

_____ _____

_____ _____

Circle the word **good**.

dog   goof

good   goal

go   goose

Circle the vowels in the word **good**.
The vowels are **a, e, i, o, u**.

g o o d

Find the set of boxes that **good** fits into. Write **good** in the correct set of boxes.

Write the word to finish this sentence.

Walking is _____

_____ for you.

SIGHT WORD

sentence

Trace the word **sentence**.

sentence

Write the word **sentence** on the lines.

Circle the word **sentence**.

tense   sense

sent   dent

tent   sentence

Circle the vowels in the word **sentence**.
The vowels are **a, e, i, o, u**.

sentence

Find the set of boxes that **sentence** fits into. Write **sentence** in the correct set of boxes.

Write the word to finish this sentence.

Can you read each

?

SIGHT WORD # man

Trace the word **man**.

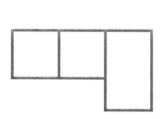

Write the word **man** on the lines.

_____ _____

_____ _____

_____ _____

Circle the word **man**.

am	map
men	mad
man	ham

Circle the vowel in the word **man**. The vowels are **a, e, i, o, u**.

m a n

Find the set of boxes that **man** fits into. Write **man** in the correct set of boxes.

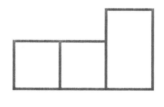

Write the word to finish this sentence.

The _____ is

going to work.

SIGHT WORD

think

Trace the word **think**.

think think

Write the word **think** on the lines.

_____ _____

_____ _____

_____ _____

Circle the word **think**.

pink   think

thin   thing

link   sink

Circle the vowel in the word **think**. The vowels are **a**, **e**, **i**, **o**, **u**.

t h i n k

Find the set of boxes that **think** fits into. Write **think** in the correct set of boxes.

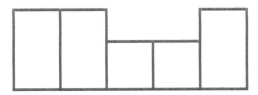
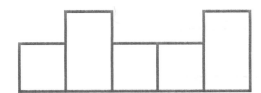

Write the word to finish this sentence.

Do you _____

she is mad?

Name _____ Date _____

SIGHT WORD

say

Trace the word **say**.

Write the word **say** on the lines.

_____ _____

_____ _____

_____ _____

Circle the word **say**.

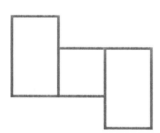

day   hay

say   lay

stay   sag

Circle the vowel in the word **say**. The vowels are **a, e, i, o, u**.

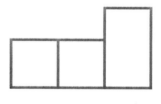

s a y

Find the set of boxes that **say** fits into. Write **say** in the correct set of boxes.

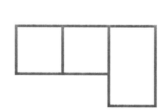

Write the word to finish this sentence.

What did the
_____
bird _____?

Peep!

Name _____ Date _____

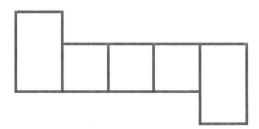

SIGHT WORD

great

Trace the word **great**.

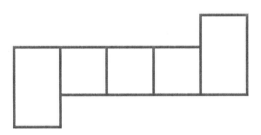

Write the word **great** on the lines.

_____ _____

Circle the word **great**.

greet   grease

treat   green

great   grade

Circle the vowels in the word **great**.
The vowels are **a**, **e**, **i**, **o**, **u**.

g r e a t

Find the set of boxes that **great** fits into. Write **great** in the correct set of boxes.

Write the word to finish this sentence.

We are having a
_____
_____ time!

Name _____ Date _____

where

Trace the word **where**.

where where

Write the word **where** on the lines.

_____ _____

_____ _____

_____ _____

Circle the word **where**.

were   when

wear   wheat

here   where

Circle the vowels in the word **where**. The vowels are **a, e, i, o, u**.

where

Find the set of boxes that **where** fits into. Write **where** in the correct set of boxes.

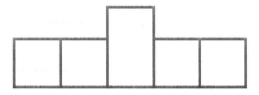   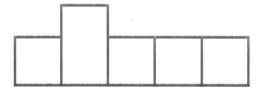

Write the word to finish this sentence.

_____

_____ did

the dog go?

SIGHT WORD

help

Trace the word **help**.

help   help

Write the word **help** on the lines.

_____   _____

_____   _____

_____   _____

_____   _____

Circle the word **help**.

heal   heel

heat   help

peel   hope

Circle the vowel in the word **help**. The vowels are **a, e, i, o, u.**

h e l p

Find the set of boxes that **help** fits into. Write **help** in the correct set of boxes.

Write the word to finish this sentence.

Can you

_____

_____ me?

Name _____   Date _____

SIGHT WORD

through

Trace the word **through**.

through

Write the word **through** on the lines.

_____

_____

_____

Circle the word **through**.

through	threw
throw	throne
thought	throat

Circle the vowels in the word **through**.
The vowels are **a, e, i, o, u.**

through

Find the set of boxes that **through** fits into. Write **through** in the correct set of boxes.

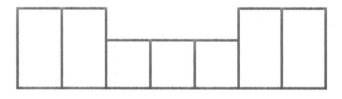   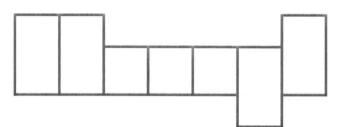

Write the word to finish this sentence.

She will walk

_____

_____

the door.

Name _____ Date _____

SIGHT WORD much

Trace the word **much**.

much much

Write the word **much** on the lines.

_____   _____

_____   _____

_____   _____

_____   _____

Circle the word **much**.

munch   much

such   lunch

mush   mouth

Circle the vowel in the word **much**.
The vowels are **a**, **e**, **i**, **o**, **u**.

m u c h

Find the set of boxes that **much** fits into. Write **much** in the correct set of boxes.

Write the word to finish this sentence.

The horse is
_____
_____
taller.

54 inches
2 inches
17 inches

Name _____   Date _____

SIGHT WORD # before

Trace the word **before**.

before

Write the word **before** on the lines.

_____
_____
_____

Circle the word **before**.

be   bore
before   beef
four   for

Circle the vowels in the word **before**.
The vowels are **a**, **e**, **i**, **o**, **u**.

before

Find the set of boxes that **before** fits into. Write **before** in the correct set of boxes.

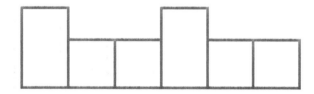 

Write the word to finish this sentence.

Brush _____

you floss!

Name _____   Date _____

line

Trace the word **line**.

line   line

Write the word **line** on the lines.

Circle the word **line**.

dine   fine

life   mine

nine   line

Circle the vowels in the word **line**. The vowels are **a, e, i, o, u**.

l i n e

Find the set of boxes that **line** fits into. Write **line** in the correct set of boxes.

Write the word to finish this sentence.

Time to

_____ up!

Name _____   Date _____

SIGHT WORD

right

Trace the word **right**.

_____

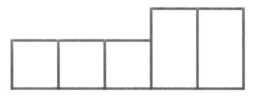

_____

Write the word **right** on the lines.

_____   _____

_____   _____

_____   _____

Circle the word **right**.

rite   rig

write   kite

right   light

Circle the vowel in the word **right**. The vowels are **a**, **e**, **i**, **o**, **u**.

r i g h t

Find the set of boxes that **right** fits into. Write **right** in the correct set of boxes.

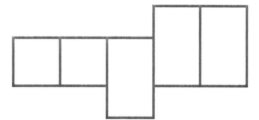

Write the word to finish this sentence.

One of its _____

legs is hurt.

SIGH WORD

too

Trace the word **too**.

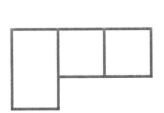

Write the word **too** on the lines.

Circle the word **too**.

two	root
toad	too
boot	foot

Circle the vowels in the word **too**. The vowels are **a, e, i, o, u.**

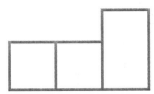

t   o   o

Find the set of boxes that **too** fits into. Write **too** in the correct set of boxes.

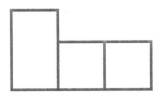

Write the word to finish this sentence.

He ate
_____
_____ much.

Name _____ Date _____

SIGHT WORD

means

Trace the word **means**.

……………………………………………

means

_____

Write the word **means** on the lines.

_____

……………………………………………

_____

……………………………………………

_____

Circle the word **means**.

meals   means

teams   beans

leans   seems

Circle the vowels in the word **means**. The vowels are **a, e, i, o, u.**

means

Find the set of boxes that **means** fits into. Write **means** in the correct set of boxes.

Write the word to finish this sentence.

_____

……………………………………………

No _____ no.

Name _____ **Date** _____

SIGHT WORD old

Trace the word **old**.

old   old

Write the word **old** on the lines.

_____ _____

_____ _____

Circle the word **old**.

old   odd

bold   gold

cold   sold

Circle the vowel in the word **old**. The vowels are **a, e, i, o, u.**

o   l   d

Find the set of boxes that **old** fits into. Write **old** in the correct set of boxes.

Write the word to finish this sentence.

This is an

_____ book.

Name _____ Date _____

SIGHT WORD

any

Trace the word **any**.

_____

....

any   any

_____

Write the word **any** on the lines.

_____   _____

....

_____   _____

_____   _____

_____   _____

Circle the word **any**.

nay   penny

candy   handy

manly   any

Circle the vowels in the word **any**. The vowels are **a**, **e**, **i**, **o**, **u**, and sometimes **y**.

a n y

Find the set of boxes that **any** fits into. Write **any** in the correct set of boxes.

Write the word to finish this sentence.

Would you like _____ .... _____ food?

SIGHT WORD

same

Trace the word **same**.

same same

Write the word **same** on the lines.

_____ _____

_____ _____

_____ _____

Circle the word **same**.

came   sang

same   sand

game   name

Circle the vowels in the word **same**.
The vowels are **a**, **e**, **i**, **o**, **u**.

s a m e

Find the set of boxes that **same** fits into. Write **same** in the correct set of boxes.

Write the word to finish this sentence.

Are these the

_____

_____ ?

Name _____   Date _____

SIGHT WORD

tell

Trace the word **tell**.

tell   tell

Write the word **tell** on the lines.

_____   _____

_____   _____

_____   _____

Circle the word **tell**.

toll   bell

teal   tell

till   fell

Circle the vowel in the word **tell**. The vowels are **a, e, i, o, u**.

t   e   l   l

Find the set of boxes that **tell** fits into. Write **tell** in the correct set of boxes.

Write the word to finish this sentence.

_____

_____

us a story.

SIGHT WORD

boy

Trace the word **boy**.

boy   boy

Write the word **boy** on the lines.

Circle the word **boy**.

toy   body

bog   coy

boy   bop

Circle the vowel in the word **boy**. The vowels are **a**, **e**, **i**, **o**, **u**.

b o y

Find the set of boxes that **boy** fits into. Write **boy** in the correct set of boxes.

Write the word to finish this sentence.

The _____ touched the flowers.

Name _____ **Date** _____

follow

Trace the word **follow**.

....
follow
....
_____

Write the word **follow** on the lines.

_____

....
_____

....
_____

Circle the word **follow**.

follow   fall

mellow   hollow

pillow   low

Circle the vowels in the word **follow**.
The vowels are **a, e, i, o, u**.

follow

Find the set of boxes that **follow** fits into. Write **follow** in the correct set of boxes.

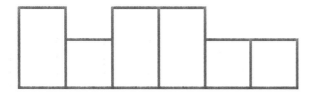

Write the word to finish this sentence.

_____

Can you ....
_____

our beat?

Name _____   Date _____

SIGHT WORD # came

Trace the word **came**.

came came

Write the word **came** on the lines.

Circle the word **came**.

same	came
come	cane
tame	cone

Circle the vowels in the word **came**.
The vowels are **a, e, i, o, u.**

c a m e

Find the set of boxes that **came** fits into. Write **came** in the correct set of boxes.

Write the word to finish this sentence.

The robot dog
_____
with a guide.

Name _____ Date _____

want

Trace the word **want**.

want want

Write the word **want** on the lines.

_____ _____

_____ _____

_____ _____

Circle the word **want**.

wait   rant

wand   tan

what   want

Circle the vowel in the word **want**.
The vowels are **a, e, i, o, u**.

w a n t

Find the set of boxes that **want** fits into. Write **want** in the correct set of boxes.

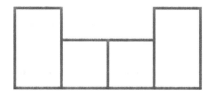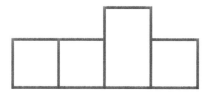

Write the word to finish this sentence.

Where do you

_____

_____ to go?

SIGHT WORD

show

Trace the word **show**.

show show

Write the word **show** on the lines.

_____   _____

_____   _____

_____   _____

Circle the word **show**.

shop   hogs

bow   show

shoe   shore

Circle the vowel in the word **show**.
The vowels are **a, e, i, o, u.**

s h o w

Find the set of boxes that **show** fits into. Write **show** in the correct set of boxes.

Write the word to finish this sentence.

Will you _____

me your book?

Name _____   Date _____

SIGHT WORD

also

Trace the word **also**.

~~also~~ ~~also~~

Write the word **also** on the lines.

_____   _____

_____   _____

_____   _____

_____   _____

Circle the word **also**.

slow   all

also   ask

salt   last

Circle the vowels in the word **also**.
The vowels are **a, e, i, o, u**.

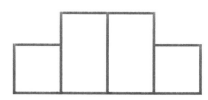

a   l   s   o

Find the set of boxes that **also** fits into. Write **also** in the correct set of boxes.

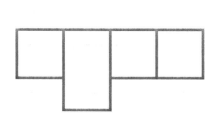   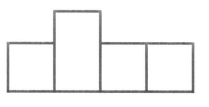   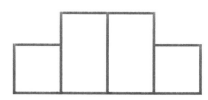

Write the word to finish this sentence.

He _____

tapped a drum.

SIGHT WORD

around

Trace the word **around**.

around

Write the word **around** on the lines.

Circle the word **around**.

around ground

arrow hound

found crowned

Circle the vowels in the word **around**.
The vowels are **a**, **e**, **i**, **o**, **u**.

around

Find the set of boxes that **around** fits into. Write **around** in the correct set of boxes.

Write the word to finish this sentence.

The dog ran

_____

_____ him.

SIGN WORD

form

Trace the word **form**.

form form

Write the word **form** on the lines.

_____   _____

_____   _____

_____   _____

Circle the word **form**.

foam   fort

fork   harm

worm   form

Circle the vowel in the word **form**. The vowels are **a, e, i, o, u**.

f o r m

Find the set of boxes that **form** fits into. Write **form** in the correct set of boxes.

Write the word to finish this sentence.

_____

What _____

do you see?

SIGHT WORD

three

Trace the word **three**.

three three

Write the word **three** on the lines.

_____ _____

_____ _____

_____ _____

_____ _____

Circle the word **three**.

fee   thread

reed   three

the   reef

Circle the vowels in the word **three**. The vowels are **a, e, i, o, u**.

t h r e e

Find the set of boxes that **three** fits into. Write **three** in the correct set of boxes.

Write the word to finish this sentence.

Do you have

_____

_____ pets?

Name _____ **Date** _____

SIGHT WORD

small

Trace the word **small**.

small small

Write the word **small** on the lines.

_____ _____

_____ _____

_____ _____

Circle the word **small**.

small	sail
snail	smart
smell	malls

Circle the vowel in the word **small**.
The vowels are **a**, **e**, **i**, **o**, **u**.

s m a l l

Find the set of boxes that **small** fits into. Write **small** in the correct set of boxes.

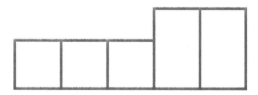 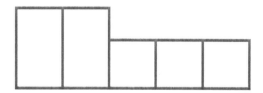

Write the word to finish this sentence.

These are
_____

_____ cubes.

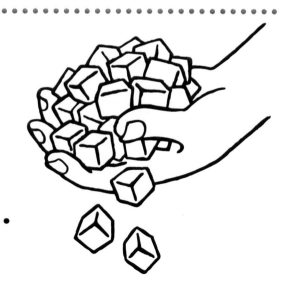

Choose the Sight Word

Circle the word that completes each sentence.

Read and trace this _____.

sentence

number

They will _____ him.

follow

through

Choose the Sight Word

Circle the word that completes each sentence.

_____ you see the owl?

Did

Our

What _____ do you hear?

before

sound

Choose the Sight Word

Circle the word that completes each sentence.

She _____ eat dinner soon.

will

then

• •

The _____ can't find his homework.

boy

its

Choose the Sight Word

Circle the word that completes each sentence.

There are _____ fish.

after

three

He _____ no money.

may

has

Choose the Sight Word

Circle the word that completes each sentence.

Do you like my _____ coat?

name

new

What does she _____?

see

means

Choose the Sight Word

Circle the word that completes each sentence.

Do you _____ to walk on the moon?

want

water

They _____ the game.

long

like

Choose the Sight Word

Circle the word that completes each sentence.

The _____ caps are dirty.

two

out

The _____ bird looks happy.

would

little

Choose the Sight Word

Circle the word that completes each sentence.

You can _____ this, too!

made

make

They play _____ well together.

very

many

Choose the Sight Word

Circle the word that completes each sentence.

Can you _____ it is windy?

tell

time

The mouse will _____ the lion.

live

help

Choose the Sight Word

Circle the word that completes each sentence.

I do not _____ he will fall.

things

think

Is this _____ you live?

where

years

    114

Choose the Sight Word

Circle the word that completes each sentence.

He is _____ at making a mess.

good

give

The fox jumped _____ the dog.

only

over

Choose the Sight Word

Circle the word that completes each sentence.

There are _____ many to eat.

get

too

Does she _____ where to go?

know

part

Name _____ Date _____

Choose the Sight Word

Circle the word that completes each sentence.

How did it get _____ there?

up

no

Plant the seeds _____.

first

other

Choose the Sight Word

Circle the word that completes each sentence.

_____ at the card I made!

Came

Look

She is marching in _____.

people

place

Choose the Sight Word

Circle the word that completes each sentence.

Did you _____ these today?

find

more

I wish I _____ jump like that.

could

come

Choose the Sight Word

Circle the word that completes each sentence.

_____ ice cream is melting.

Him

Her

_____ will order first?

Way

Who

Flash Cards

will	many	some
up	then	her
other	them	would
about	these	make
out	so	like

Flash Cards *(cont.)*

him	two	number
into	more	no
time	write	way
has	go	could
look	see	people

Flash Cards *(cont.)*

my	called	find
than	who	long
first	am	down
water	its	day
been	now	did

Flash Cards *(cont.)*

get	over	little
come	new	work
made	sound	know
may	take	place
part	only	years

Flash Cards *(cont.)*

live	very	name
me	after	good
back	things	sentence
give	our	man
most	just	think

Flash Cards (cont.)

say	much	means
great	before	old
where	line	any
help	right	same
through	too	tell

Flash Cards *(cont.)*

boy	also
follow	around
came	form
want	three
show	small

Meeting Standards

Each activity meets the following Common Core State Standards © Copyright 2010. National Governors Association Center for Best Practices and Council of Chief State School Officers. All rights reserved. For more information about the Common Core State Standards, go to *http://www.corestandards.org/* or *http://www.teachercreated.com/ standards/*.

Grade 1	
Reading: Foundational Skills	**Pages**
Print Concepts	
ELA.RF.1.1: Demonstrate understanding of the organization and basic features of print.	5–54
Phonics and Word Recognition	
ELA.RF.1.3: Know and apply grade-level phonics and word analysis skills in decoding words.	5–54, 105–120
Language	**Pages**
Conventions of Standard English	
ELA.L.1.2: Demonstrate command of the conventions of standard English capitalization, punctuation, and spelling when writing.	5–54

Grade 2	
Reading: Foundational Skills	**Pages**
Phonics and Word Recognition	
ELA.RF.2.3: Know and apply grade-level phonics and word analysis skills in decoding words.	55–120
Language	**Pages**
Conventions of Standard English	
ELA.L.2.2: Demonstrate command of the conventions of standard English capitalization, punctuation, and spelling when writing.	55–104